LUNCH WITH LO♥E

Daily Love Notes to Cut, Share and surprise at Mealtime

By Magdalena Murphy

WTL INTERNATIONAL

LUNCH WITH LOVE

Copyright © 2025 Magdalena Murphy

All rights reserved. No part of this publication may be reproduced
in any form or by any electronic or mechanical means, including information storage
and material systems, except in the case of brief quotations embodied in critical
articles or reviews, without permission
in writing from its publisher,
WTL International.

Published by
WTL International
930 North Park Drive
P.O. Box 33049
Brampton, Ontario
L6S 6A7 Canada
www.wtlipublishing.com

978-1-927865-35-4

DEDICATION...

I WOULD LIKE TO DEDICATE THIS BOOK TO MY CHILDREN, BRIAN AND OLA.

"I WILL LOVE YOU FOREVER..."

XOXO

M.

BE KIND TO YOURSELF FIRST! THEN LET YOUR KINDNESS FILL THE WORLD.

xoxo

LUNCH WITH LO♥E

HELP
SOMEONE
TODAY.
xoxo

LUNCH WITH LO♥E

THE WORLD IS
A BETTER PLACE
BECAUSE
YOU'RE IN IT!

xoxo

LUNCH WITH LO♡E

BE SOMEBODY
WHO MAKES
EVERYBODY FEEL
LIKE SOMEBODY.
       XOXO

LUNCH WITH LO♡E

SELF-KINDNESS IS WHEN YOU BECOME YOUR OWN COACH INSTEAD OF YOUR CRITIC.

xoxo

LUNCH WITH LO♡E

IF YOU ARE ALWAYS TRYING TO BE "NORMAL," YOU'LL NEVER KNOW HOW AMAZING YOU CAN BE!

XOXO

LUNCH WITH LO♥E

IN THE WORLD,
WHERE YOU CAN
BE ANYTHING,
BE YOURSELF!

XOXO

LUNCH WITH LO♥E

EVERY CHILD MATTERS.

xoxo

LUNCH WITH LO♡E

"IN SCHOOL, YOU LEARN THE LESSON, THEN TAKE THE TEST. IN LIFE, YOU HAVE THE TEST FIRST, THEN YOU FIGURE OUT THE LESSON IT'S TRYING TO TEACH YOU AFTERWARDS."
~KWAME OSEI

XOXO

LUNCH WITH LO♥E

DON'T JUST BE GOOD TO OTHERS. BE GOOD TO YOURSELF TOO.

XOXO

LUNCH WITH LO♡E

TALK TO YOURSELF LIKE YOU WOULD TO SOMEONE YOU LOVE.

xoxo

LUNCH WITH LO♡E

"A FRIEND IS SOMEONE WHO GIVES YOU TOTAL FREEDOM TO BE YOURSELF."
~JIM MORRISON

XOXO

LUNCH WITH LO♥E

CONFIDENCE ISN'T THINKING YOU ARE BETTER THAN EVERYONE ELSE, IT'S REALIZING THAT YOU HAVE NO REASON TO COMPARE YOURSELF TO ANYONE ELSE.

XOXO

LUNCH WITH LO♡E

No amount of regret changes the past.
No amount of anxiety changes the future...
Any amount of gratitude changes the present.

xoxo

LUNCH WITH LO♡E

IT'S HEALTHY TO ADMIT YOU'RE NOT OKAY.
IT'S BRAVE TO BE SAD BUT DON'T LET SADNESS WIN.
XOXO

LUNCH WITH LO♥E

YOUR MIND IS A GARDEN. YOUR THOUGHTS ARE THE SEEDS. YOU CAN GROW FLOWERS OR YOU CAN GROW WEEDS.

XOXO

LUNCH WITH LO♥E

YOU CAN BE A GOOD PERSON WITH A KIND HEART AND STILL SAY NO.

XOXO

LUNCH WITH LO♡E

"People will forget what you said. People will forget what you did, but people will never forget how you made them feel."
~Maya Angelou

xoxo

LUNCH WITH LO♥E

NOT EVERY DAY
MAY BE GOOD,
BUT
THERE IS GOOD
IN EVERY DAY!
xoxo

LUNCH WITH LO♥E

THE SMALLEST ACT OF KINDNESS IS WORTH MORE THAN THE GRANDEST INTENTION.

XOXO

LUNCH WITH LO♥E

"THERE IS ALWAYS LIGHT, IF ONLY WE'RE BRAVE ENOUGH TO SEE IT. IF ONLY WE ARE BRAVE ENOUGH TO BE IT!"

~AMANDA GORMAN

XOXO

LUNCH WITH LO♡E

IF YOU DO WHAT IS EASY, YOUR LIFE WILL BE HARD. IF YOU DO WHAT IS HARD, YOUR LIFE WILL BE EASY.

xoxo

LUNCH WITH LO♥E

"There are better things ahead than any we leave behind."
~C. S. Lewis

xoxo

LUNCH WITH LO♥E

"Darkness cannot drive out darkness; only light can do that. Hate cannot drive out hate; only love can do that."

~Dr. Martin Luther King Jr.

xoxo

LUNCH WITH LO♡E

NEVER APOLOGIZE FOR SHOWING FEELINGS. WHEN YOU DO SO, YOU ARE APOLOGIZING FOR TRUTH.

XOXO

LUNCH WITH LO♡E

"A PERSON WHO NEVER MADE A MISTAKE NEVER TRIED ANYTHING NEW."
~ALBERT EINSTEIN

XOXO

LUNCH WITH LO♡E

TWO OF THE MOST IMPORTANT DAYS IN YOUR LIFE ARE THE DAY YOU WERE BORN AND THE DAY YOU FIND OUT WHY.

XOXO

LUNCH WITH LO♡E

'I AM SORRY.
FORGIVE ME.
THANK YOU.
I LOVE YOU.'
~HO'OPONOPONO
PRAYER

                        XOXO

LUNCH WITH LO♥E

BE GOOD TO
PEOPLE FOR NO
REASON.

XOXO

LUNCH WITH LO♡E

DON'T YOU DARE SHRINK YOURSELF FOR SOMEONE ELSE'S COMFORT.

XOXO

LUNCH WITH LO♡E

WHY FIT IN WHEN YOU WERE BORN TO STAND OUT?
~DR. SEUSS

XOXO

LUNCH WITH LO♡E

WHEN YOU LOVE
WHAT YOU HAVE,
YOU HAVE
EVERYTHING
YOU NEED.

XOXO

LUNCH WITH LO♡E

IMAGINE BEING SO KIND THAT OTHERS LOVE THEMSELVES IN YOUR COMPANY.

XOXO

LUNCH WITH LO♡E

IF YOU ARE NOT WILLING TO LEARN, NO ONE CAN HELP YOU. IF YOU ARE DETERMINED TO LEARN, NO ONE CAN STOP YOU.

XOXO

LUNCH WITH LO♥E

IF YOU THINK YOU'RE TOO SMALL TO MAKE AN IMPACT, THEN YOU HAVEN'T BEEN IN A ROOM WITH A MOSQUITO!

XOXO

LUNCH WITH LO♡E

ONE DAY YOU WILL FIND SOMEONE THAT IS OBSESSED WITH YOU! IT'S PROBABLY GOING TO BE A DOG... BUT IT IS WHAT IT IS!

XOXO

LUNCH WITH LO♥E

A FLOWER DOES NOT THINK OF COMPETING WITH THE FLOWER NEXT TO IT.
IT JUST BLOOMS.

XOXO

LUNCH WITH LO♡E

INSTEAD OF USING YOUR ENERGY TO WORRY, USE YOUR ENERGY TO BELIEVE.

XOXO

LUNCH WITH LO♡E

ONE SHALL
POSITIVE THOUGHT
IN THE MORNING
CAN CHANGE YOUR
WHOLE DAY.

XOXO

LUNCH WITH LO♡E

BE CAREFUL HOW YOU ARE TALKING TO YOURSELF BECAUSE YOU ARE LISTENING.

XOXO

LUNCH WITH LO♥E

THE SECRET TO HAPPINESS IS TO COUNT YOUR BLESSINGS WHILE OTHERS ARE ADDING UP THEIR TROUBLES.

XOXO

LUNCH WITH LO♡E

YOU ARE
AWESOME!
XOXO

LUNCH WITH LO♥E

NEVER WAIT FOR A PERFECT MOMENT, JUST TAKE A MOMENT AND MAKE IT PERFECT.

xoxo

LUNCH WITH LO♡E

MAGIC IS BELIEVING IN YOURSELF. IF YOU CAN MAKE THAT HAPPEN, YOU CAN MAKE ANYTHING HAPPEN.
XOXO

LUNCH WITH LO♥E

MAY YOU LIVE AS LONG AS YOU LIKE AND ENJOY WHAT YOU LIKE AS LONG AS YOU LIVE!

xoxo

LUNCH WITH LO♡E

EVERY DAY IS A
FRESH START.
xoxo

LUNCH WITH LO♥E

TODAY IS GOING TO BE AWESOME!

xoxo

LUNCH WITH LO♡E

TO SHARE YOUR HEAKNESS IS TO MAKE YOURSELF VULNERABLE. TO MAKE YOURSELF VULNERABLE IS TO SHOW YOUR STRENGTH.

XOXO

LUNCH WITH LO♥E

FORGET ALL THE REASONS IT WON'T WORK AND BELIEVE THE ONE REASON THAT IT WILL.

XOXO

LUNCH WITH LO♥E

WORDS MATTER, AND THE WORDS THAT MATTER MOST ARE THE ONES YOU SAY TO YOURSELF!

XOXO

LUNCH WITH LO♡E

"How many years has it taken people to realize... we are all brothers and sisters and human beings in the human race?"
~Marsha P. Johnson

xoxo

LUNCH WITH LO♡E

WAKE UP.
KICK BUTT.
BE KIND.
REPEAT.

xoxo

LUNCH WITH LO♥E

YOU OWE YOURSELF THE LOVE THAT YOU SO FREELY GIVE TO OTHER PEOPLE.

XOXO

LUNCH WITH LO♥E

Do what feels good. Follow what brings you joy. Find excitement and laughter... You are worthy of being light, happy and free!

xoxo

LUNCH WITH LO♥E

TALKING ABOUT OUR PROBLEMS IS OUR GREATEST ADDICTION. BREAK THE HABIT. TALK ABOUT YOUR JOYS.

XOXO

LUNCH WITH LO♡E

IF YOU SEE SOMETHING BEAUTIFUL IN SOMEONE, SPEAK IT.

XOXO

LUNCH WITH LO♥E

STOP COMPARING YOURSELF. FLOWERS ARE PRETTY, BUT SO ARE SUNSETS, AND THEY LOOK NOTHING ALIKE.

XOXO

LUNCH WITH LO♡E

I LOVE YOU!
xoxo

LUNCH WITH LO♡E

WHEN YOU NEED SOMETHING TO BELIEVE IN, START WITH YOURSELF.

XOXO

LUNCH WITH LO♥E

YOUR THOUGHTS SET THE COURSE FOR YOUR DAY, BUT YOU CAN SET THE COURSE FOR YOUR THOUGHTS.

xoxo

LUNCH WITH LO♥E

HAPPINESS IS BY <u>CHOICE</u> NOT BY CHANCE.

XOXO

LUNCH WITH LO♥E

TODAY I CHOOSE CALM OVER CHAOS, SERENITY OVER STRESS, PEACE OVER PERFECTION, GRACE OVER GRIT, FAITH OVER FEAR.

XOXO

LUNCH WITH LO♡E

YOU HAVE THE POWER TO SAY, "THIS IS NOT HOW MY STORY WILL END."

XOXO

LUNCH WITH LO♡E

LET YOUR SMILE CHANGE THE WORLD BUT DON'T LET THE WORLD CHANGE YOUR SMILE!

XOXO

LUNCH WITH LO♡E

LIFE IS 10% WHAT HAPPENS TO YOU AND 90% HOW YOU REACT TO IT.

xoxo

LUNCH WITH LO♥E

YOU WILL NEVER BE HAPPY IF YOU ARE CONSTANTLY JUDGING YOURSELF. GIVE YOURSELF SOME GRACE.

XOXO

LUNCH WITH LO♡E

When you stop expecting people to be perfect, you can like them for who they are.

xoxo

LUNCH WITH LO♡E

WHEN YOU FOCUS ON THE GOOD, THE GOOD GETS BETTER.

xoxo

LUNCH WITH LO♥E

LOVE YOURSELF
AS MUCH AS YOU
WANT TO BE
LOVED.
                    XOXO

LUNCH WITH LO♡E

YOU ARE VALUABLE BECAUSE YOU EXIST, NOT BECAUSE OF WHAT YOU DO OR WHAT YOU HAVE DONE... BUT SIMPLY BECAUSE <u>YOU ARE</u>

xoxo

LUNCH WITH LO♡E

"TRUST THAT THE UNIVERSE IS WORKING FOR YOU AND WITH YOU."
~SANAYA ROMAN

XOXO

LUNCH WITH LO♥E

"A THING OF BEAUTY IS A JOY FOR EVER..."
~JOHN KEATS

xoxo

LUNCH WITH LO♥E

YOU ARE
PERFECT JUST
THE WAY
YOU ARE.

XOXO

LUNCH WITH LO♥E

YOU HAVE
UNLIMITED
CREATIVITY.
THAT'S YOUR
SUPERPOWER.
XOXO

LUNCH WITH LO♥E

I AM GRATEFULL
FOR YOU.
xoxo

LUNCH WITH LO♡E

"KIND WORDS CAN BE SHORT AND EASY TO SPEAK, BUT THEIR ECHOES ARE TRULY ENDLESS."
~MOTHER TERESA

XOXO

LUNCH WITH LO♥E

"DON'T EVER BE ASHAMED OF LOVING THE STRANGE THINGS THAT MAKE YOUR WEIRD LITTLE HEART HAPPY."

~ELIZABETH GILBERT

XOXO

LUNCH WITH LO♥E

THERE IS SO MUCH PEACE IN KNOWING YOU WILL NOT MISS OUT ON WHAT'S MEANT FOR YOU!

XOXO

LUNCH WITH LO♡E

STOP USING YOUR ENERGY TO WORRY. USE YOUR ENERGY TO BELIEVE, CREATE, LOVE, GROW, GLOW, MANIFEST AND HEAL.

XOXO

LUNCH WITH LO♥E

"Everything is going to be okay in the end. If it's not the okay, it's not the end."
~John Lennon

xoxo

LUNCH WITH LO♥E

WHAT DO YOU
LOVE DOING?
               XOXO

LUNCH WITH LO♡E

KNOW THAT DEEP DOWN INSIDE YOU ARE RESILIENCE AND BRAVERY, AND YOU ARE SO MUCH STRONGER AND MORE POWERFUL THAN YOUR FEARS.

XOXO

LUNCH WITH LO♥E

LOVE YOURSELF SO MUCH THAT WHEN SOMEONE TREATS YOU WRONG, YOU RECOGNIZE IT.

XOXO

LUNCH WITH LO♡E

THE DARKEST NIGHTS PRODUCE THE BRIGHTEST STARS.

xoxo

LUNCH WITH LO♡E

BE WHO YOU ARE AND SAY WHAT YOU FEEL, BECAUSE THOSE WHO MIND DON'T MATTER AND THOSE WHO MATTER DON'T MIND.
~DR. SEUSS

xoxo

LUNCH WITH LO♥E

I AM HEALTHY.
xoxo

LUNCH WITH LO♡E

I AM LOVED.
xoxo

LUNCH WITH LO♥E

I AM HAPPY.

    XOXO

LUNCH WITH LO♥E

3 THINGS THAT MAKE ME HAPPY

1.

2.

3.

XOXO

LUNCH WITH LO♥E

"BE THE CHANGE
YOU WANT
TO SEE
IN THE WORLD."
~M. GANDHI

                XOXO

LUNCH WITH LO♡E

I AM THE HERO
OF MY LIFE.
xoxo

LUNCH WITH LO♥E

THANK YOU FOR
BEING YOU!
             XOXO

LUNCH WITH LO♡E

WHAT YOU ARE DRAWN TO IS INSEPARABLY CONNECTED TO YOUR PURPOSE. LISTEN TO YOUR INTUITION.

XOXO

LUNCH WITH LO♥E

YOU ARE MY
SUNSHINE.
xoxo

LUNCH WITH LO♥E

"IT'S IMPOSSIBLE,"
SAID PRIDE.
"IT'S RISKY," SAID
EXPERIENCE.
"IT'S POINTLESS,"
SAID REASON.
"GIVE IT A TRY,"
WHISPERED
THE HEART.

XOXO

LUNCH WITH LO♡E

DON'T CHANGE YOURSELF JUST TO MAKE SOMEONE HAPPY, UNLESS THAT SOMEONE IS YOU.

XOXO

LUNCH WITH LO♥E

BE...
YOU.

XOXO

LUNCH WITH LO♥E

To accomplish great things, we must not only act, but also dream; not only plan, but also believe.

xoxo

LUNCH WITH LO♡E

I'LL LOVE YOU FOREVER. I'LL LIKE YOU FOR ALWAYS. AS LONG AS I'M LIVING, MY BABY YOU'LL BE!

~R. MUNSCH

XOXO

LUNCH WITH LO♥E

PLACE YOUR HAND OVER YOUR HEART. CAN YOU FEEL IT? THAT'S CALLED "PURPOSE." YOU ARE ALIVE FOR A REASON, SO DON'T EVER GIVE UP.

XOXO

LUNCH WITH LO♥E

I ♡ you.
xoxo

LUNCH WITH LO♥E

"NEVER HAVE REGRETS. FOLLOW YOUR HEART."
~UNKNOWN

XOXO

LUNCH WITH LO♥E

YOU MAKE THE WORLD A BETTER PLACE.

XOXO

LUNCH WITH LO♥E

DON'T MAKE YOURSELF
SMALL FOR ANYONE.
BE THE AWKWARD,
FUNNY, INTELLIGENT,
BEAUTIFUL, CREATIVE
SOUL THAT YOU ARE.
DON'T HOLD BACK.

       XOXO

LUNCH WITH LO♥E

YOU'RE SO LOVED!
XOXO

LUNCH WITH LO♡E

"BEING HONEST MAY NOT GET YOU A LOT OF FRIENDS BUT IT'LL ALWAYS GET YOU THE RIGHT ONES."
~JOHN LENNON

XOXO

LUNCH WITH LO♥E

"Carry out an act of kindness with no expectation of reward, safe in the knowledge that one day someone might do the same to you."
~Princess Diana

xoxo

LUNCH WITH LO♡E

CELEBRATE FRIENDSHIPS THAT EMPOWER YOU TO BE THE MOST AUTHENTIC SELF.

XOXO

LUNCH WITH LO♡E

I LOVE PEOPLE THAT HAVE NO IDEA HOW WONDERFUL THEY ARE AND JUST WANDER AROUND MAKING THE WORLD A BETTER PLACE.
I LOVE YOU!

XOXO

LUNCH WITH LO♥E

May your troubles be less and your blessings be more, and nothing but happiness come through your door.

xoxo

LUNCH WITH LO♡E

EVERYONE YOU MEET IS FIGHTING A BATTLE YOU KNOW NOTHING ABOUT.
BE KIND ALWAYS.

XOXO

LUNCH WITH LO♥E

MAYBE THE JOURNEY ISN'T SO MUCH ABOUT BECOMING ANYTHING. MAYBE IT'S ABOUT UN-BECOMING EVERYTHING THAT ISN'T REALLY YOU.

XOXO

LUNCH WITH LO♥E

I CANNOT MAKE YOU HAPPY BUT I CAN COMMIT TO SUPPORTING YOU IN THE CREATION OF YOUR OWN HAPPINESS.

XOXO

LUNCH WITH LO♡E

TODAY I GIVE THANKS FOR ALL THINGS IN MY LIFE THAT DON'T NEED FIXING.

XOXO

LUNCH WITH LO♥E

"Without faith, nothing is possible. With it, nothing is impossible."
~Mary McLeod Bethune

xoxo

LUNCH WITH LO♥E

HAPPINESS IS LETTING GO OF WHAT YOU THINK YOUR LIFE IS SUPPOSED TO LOOK LIKE AND CELEBRATING IT FOR EVERYTHING THAT IT IS.

XOXO

LUNCH WITH LO♥E

THINGS TO BE
GRATEFUL FOR:
- WHAT LEFT
- WHAT STAYED
- WHAT'S ON
  THE WAY

XOXO

LUNCH WITH LO♥E

TO BE BEAUTIFUL MEANS TO BE YOURSELF. YOU DON'T NEED TO BE ACCEPTED BY OTHERS. YOU NEED TO ACCEPT YOURSELF.

XOXO

LUNCH WITH LO♥E

WHAT THEY HATE
IN YOU IS MISSING
IN THEM.
KEEP SHINING.
              XOXO

LUNCH WITH LO♡E

THE MOST IMPORTANT DAY IS THE DAY YOU DECIDE YOU'RE GOOD ENOUGH FOR YOU. IT'S THE DAY YOU SET YOURSELF FREE.

xoxo

LUNCH WITH LO♡E

BE HAPPY WITH
WHAT YOU HAVE
AND YOU WILL
HAVE PLENTY TO
BE HAPPY ABOUT.
XOXO

LUNCH WITH LO♥E

NEXT TIME SOMEONE
TRIES TO BRING YOU
DOWN, REMEMBER:
CONFIDENCE
IS QUIET;
INSECURITY IS LOUD.
                    XOXO

LUNCH WITH LO♥E

Your mind will believe what you continuously tell it. So tell it that you are smart, talented, kind, fearless, and you have what it takes.

xoxo

LUNCH WITH LO♡E

SOME STRANGER SOMEWHERE STILL REMEMBERS YOU BECAUSE YOU WERE KIND TO THEM WHEN NO ONE ELSE HAS.

xoxo

LUNCH WITH LO♡E

WHAT YOU ARE LOOKING FOR IS LOOKING FOR YOU.
XOXO

LUNCH WITH LO♡E

1. BE...
2. DO...
3. HAVE...

xoxo

LUNCH WITH LO♥E

ENCOURAGING SOMEONE TO BE ENTIRELY THEMSELF IS THE LOUDEST WAY TO LOVE THEM.

xoxo

LUNCH WITH LO♡E

IF YOU BELIEVE IT
WILL WORK OUT,
YOU WILL SEE
OPPORTUNITIES.
IF YOU BELIEVE IT
WON'T, YOU WILL
SEE OBSTACLES.

XOXO

LUNCH WITH LO♥E

I AM ENOUGH, AND I DON'T HAVE TO PROVE IT. I AM BECAUSE I AM —IN ALL WAYS— ALWAYS.

xoxo

LUNCH WITH LO♡E

MOST PEOPLE NEED LOVE AND ACCEPTANCE MUCH MORE THAN THEY NEED ADVICE.

XOXO

LUNCH WITH LO♡E

WHAT'S THE BEST
THAT CAN HAPPEN?
XOXO

LUNCH WITH LO♥E

LIFE IS PREPARING
YOU FOR ALL
THE MIRACLES
COMING YOUR WAY.
XOXO

LUNCH WITH LO♥E

YOU GROW FASTER WHEN YOU TAKE YOUR TIME.
XOXO

LUNCH WITH LO♡E

"WHAT IS NOW PROVED WAS ONCE ONLY IMAGINED."
~WILLIAM BLAKE

xoxo

LUNCH WITH LO♥E

"Unexpected kindness is the most powerful, least costly, and most underrated agent of human change."

~Bob Kerrey

xoxo

LUNCH WITH LO♥E

FEAR IS
"WHAT IF?"
FAITH IS
"EVEN IF."

xoxo

LUNCH WITH LO♡E

OPTIMISTS LIVE LONGER, EVEN IF THEY'RE WRONG.

xoxo

LUNCH WITH LO♥E

WE DON'T SEE THINGS AS THEY ARE; WE SEE THEM AS WE ARE.
XOXO

LUNCH WITH LO♥E

NOT ALL WHO
WANDER ARE
LOST.

xoxo

LUNCH WITH LO♡E

"EVERY TIME YOU'RE GIVEN A CHOICE BETWEEN DISAPPOINTING SOMEONE ELSE AND DISAPPOINTING YOURSELF, YOUR DUTY IS TO DISAPPOINT THAT SOMEONE ELSE. YOUR JOB, THROUGHOUT YOUR ENTIRE LIFE IS TO DISAPPOINT AS MANY PEOPLE AS IT TAKES TO AVOID DISAPPOINTING YOURSELF."
~GLENNON DOYLE "UNTAMED"

XOXO

LUNCH WITH LO♡E

About the Author

Magdalena Murphy was born and raised in Poland and has also lived in France, Switzerland and Canada.

She loves travelling, being surrounded by nature, walking, reading, fishing, fixing things and inspiring people with kindness.

The idea for this book came after hearing from her daughter that her friends were looking forward to seeing what note she had in her lunch every day!

www.ingramcontent.com/pod-product-compliance
Lightning Source LLC
Chambersburg PA
CBHW081441070526
44586CB00019B/2190